TAKING WORDS FOR A WALK

NEW AND SELECTED POEMS

ALSO BY RALPH THOMPSON

The Denting of Wave
Moving On
View from Mount Diablo
View from Mount Diablo Annotated Edition

TAKING WORDS FOR A WALK

NEW AND SELECTED POEMS

RALPH THOMPSON

PEEPAL TREE

First published in Great Britain in 2012
Peepal Tree Press
17 King's Avenue
Leeds LS6 IQS
England

ISBN 13: 9781845231958

ACKNOWLEDGEMENTS

Some of these poems originally appeared in *Ariel* (Canada), *The Mississippi Review, The Caribbean Writer, London Magazine,* the *Dulwich Poetry Festival anthology, The Oxford Book of Caribbean Verse*, *The Heinemann Book of Caribbean Poetry*, *Bearing Witness* (The best of the Observer Arts Magazine), *Calabash Anthology.*

Supported by
ARTS COUNCIL
ENGLAND

CONTENTS

Introduction 9

NEW POEMS

Taking Words for a Walk 19
Rain Forest House 20
My Uncle, the Bishop 22
Straight from the Horse's Mouth 23
The Ice Cream Bucket 25
Seasons 26
Leaf Raker 27
Truth and Consequences 28
Regret 30
Feature 31
That Time of Day 33
Wedding Flowers 34
Hooray for Grey 35
Boston Bay 36
Older at Terra Nova Hotel 37
Aubade 38
Viewpoint 39
Talbot Thwiggs 40
Lady in a Black Half-Slip 41
Tour of Duty 42
Same Old Story 43
Prophecy 44
Alarum 46
Construction 47
Constriction 48
Search 49
The Lunatic 50
The Emperor of Possibilities 51
Some Other Things that go Bump in the Night 52
Final Flight 53

Sea Anemones 54
On the Retirement of an Airline Pilot 55
First a Green Leaf 56
Elegy for my Father 57
The Day may Come 59
I have not scorned my life 60
Elegy 61
Death Wish 62
Haiku Variations 63
Strategies 64
Introduction to a Book of Photographs 65
Broom Man 66
Pride and Prejudice 67
Red Bird 68
Roots 69
A Brief Biography 70
A Terrible True Tale 71
Valley of Decision 73
Recovery 74
Noel 75
Lessons 76
Brown Sugar 77
End Game 78
Lift Off 79
Espousals 80
It's a Deal 81
The Colour of Conscience 82

Poems Previously Published

from *View From Mount Diablo* (2003)

Prologue 93
Jamaica Gothic 96

from *Moving On* (1998)

Mister Son 99
Early Encounter with the British Raj 100
Goodbye Aristotle, So Long America (Section VIII) 102
Outside the Artist's Studio 103
Vigil 104
The Garden 105
A Death in the Family 106
Third World 108
Mountain Time 109
A Long Productive Life 110
Capricorn 112
Good Friday in a Tourist Town 114
Hic Est 115
History Anyone? 117
Stephanie 118

from *The Denting of a Wave* (1992)

Carpenters 121
Ablutions 123
Harbour View 125
Jamaica Farewell 126
Waiting 127
Time and Tide 128
He Knows What Height Is 129
Death of a Honda Rider 131
Silence 132
from Mr. Goodman's Last Visit Abroad 134
Florida 135
The Virgin Mary at Wellesley College 136
Sufficiencies 139
My God 138
Cavafy at Terra Nova 140
Leda 142

EDWARD BAUGH

INTRODUCTION TO *TAKING WORDS FOR A WALK*

This collection offers a generous gift of new poems that enhance Ralph Thompson's stature in the craft. That stature has been steadily established over the last twenty years, from *The Denting of a Wave* (1992), through *Moving On* (1998), to the narrative feat of *A View from Mount Diablo* (2003). The new poems are enough to make a satisfying volume on their own, and they account for well over half of the total in *Taking Words for a Walk*. However, it is good to have a selection from the earlier books here, and not only to refresh delight in them. We may appreciate the new pieces all the more as we hear them speak to and extend the earlier pieces, and hear the Thompson voice continuing to be true to itself.

The distinctiveness of that voice announces itself in the opening poem, which provides an ideal title for the volume as it sounds the note of the poet's gently self-deprecating sense of his own negotiations with the practice of poetry. There is the characteristic whimsy of image and idea as they frolic with each other. The play is a satisfying end in itself, but it also underscores a serious point about poetry: that, contrary to what the poet may think, he does not control the poem; it is, rather, the poem that leads him into unforeseen turns and tangents and even, at times, eludes him, leaves him behind. The unexpected but entirely apposite ending, with the poet/dog-owner staring at the "empty leash", is an instance of Thompson's sense for the shape of the poem. There is the characteristic delight in irreverence, and in poetry's capacity for it, as the dog tugs itself away from the straight and narrow path to pee on the wheel of a Mercedes Benz.

The humour and whimsy take diverting turns through the collection, from, for instance, the deservedly popular "Early Encounter with the British Raj" to the cutting criticism of "Pride and

Prejudice" and the wry, dry humour of "Talbot Thwiggs". All three probe sharply the ills and frictions of relationships, whether personal or social. In "The Early Encounter" there is the bizarre, hilariously sweet "colonial revenge" served on the British soldiers parading imperially. The incongruity of the boy on the donkey, who has wandered into the stiff-upper-lip ceremony, is nicely complicated by, for instance, the comic figure of black Mr Byrd, "pre-independence social provocateur", trying ineffectively to gain entrance by pulling rank. We chuckle at how he is put down by the Cockney insult of the corporal manning the gate. There is also amusing but pertinent point in the fact that, whereas the officious Byrd may be so easily lorded over by the Limey corporal because he is black, the boy can get away with disrupting the parade because, though local and himself only an insignificant colonial subject, he is white.

"Pride and Prejudice" exposes its white-liberal "minor poet" and his condescending, predictably anti-climactic adventure into marriage with a black, hopefully exotic, Caribbean woman:

> On his return to Minnesota
> he told his friends she had left him
> for a black man better hung.
> And they believed him.

Having failed at his adventure, he takes refuge in the stereotyping prejudice of the birds of his feather. Talbot Thwiggs – and we note the comic-book name – is a born loser. In the forty-fifth year of a respectable, straight-laced and obviously shallow marriage, he tells his prim, bossy wife that he is thinking of buying a dog. She cannot imagine why he would ever want to do such a thing. When he explains, hesitantly, '"Dogs romp, wag / their tails when you talk to them, / kiss your hands, your face",' it would never occur to her to read the hint, however unconscious it may be: '"I never heard such nonsense," / she exclaims. "Hurry up / or we'll be late for church."'

Over against the cheerlessness of the Thwiggs marriage, there are poems that celebrate happily realized love, such as "Boston Bay", "The Day May Come" and a fine poem of married love, "Waiting". There are other poems too that record personal landmark moments of deep feeling and illumination, moments in some cases beyond words, liminal: "That Time of Day", "Elegy for My Father", "The Virgin Mary at Wellesley College", and "Good Friday in a Tourist Town".

An appreciable number of the poems relive childhood memories and the experience of growing up, of learning prejudice and sexuality and the way the world is; the oddities of personal family relationships and the sometimes uneasy interface between the worldviews of child and adult. For instance, "The Ice Cream Bucket" preserves a snippet of bygone Jamaican family life, the occasional evening treat, eagerly anticipated by the children, of ice-cream made in the hand-turned bucket, and the delight of the child who gets to lick the "paddle" clean when the ice-cream has been ladled out. The near-sensual delight of the licking sends "concupiscence flaring". In the instant recollection, the sociological factor is integral. The setting is "the clean dirt / of a Jamaican back-yard compacted / by the bare soles of black servants / and the shod feet of white children / in their care." The bucket is turned by the black gardener (who never gets to lick the leavings on the paddle).

These stories from childhood sometimes illustrate social, public issues of colour, class, economic deprivation, the interaction between them, and the violence which may attend that interaction. These factors complicate the poet's sense of deep attachment to his island and the "light that [he has] so long loved" ("Prologue"). Most of these concerns are active in the most recent poem in the collection, "The Colour of Conscience". The title foregrounds the theme of colour and how it affects the poet's knowledge of himself and his relationship to others.

The narrative, an easily unfolding sequence of remembered, fictionalized events and characters, features two sets of relationships, those between the narrator's mother and the generality of blacks, whether "the barefoot, uneducated masses" or her son's school friends, and those between the narrator and those friends or his domestic servants in his adulthood. There are ironic, ostensible contradictions. The poem begins,

We were poor, enjoyed no social status
and Mother, motivated by what passes
for enlightenment, never failed to teach us
scorn for the barefoot, uneducated masses.

Her son's "black school mates were not allowed inside / our house", and so he had to meet them in the garage. Although, in her basic kind-heartedness and sense of *noblesse oblige*, "no beggar for a drink was turned away", the drink was proffered "in a special glass / reserved for black lips".

Remarkably, though, when her black doctor makes an urgently requested house call, he is treated almost obsequiously, "like an African prince"; the "toilet usually acceptable for others / was attacked with scrub brush and Lysol, made fit / for the great man's ass." Thompson's irreverent humour again! Then, the mother's essential goodness shows itself in a tender, moving mother-and-son moment between her and the black deaf-mute, Aston, who sews canvas awnings for her small business. This moment made a lasting, secret impression on the boy, who happened to witness it, and who now, at last, can find the skill to fix it in poetry.

No doubt that moment played a part in his becoming a man who does not continue his mother's socialized scorn of black people in general, and who, along with his wife, treats his long-serving, live-in domestic helper, Carmen, and her daughter, Eunice, with "conscience", respect and generosity. However, the bonds of class socialization are hard to break, and more so for Carmen and Eunice. When the latter, still at high school and doing well, becomes pregnant at fifteen, "father unknown", she withdraws into sullenness, "refusing to return to school, / determined not to work, a troubled victim / of her blackness." "Carmen's heart / cracked with a remembered grief." However, over against the disappointment and perplexity, there resonate moments of simple, natural humanity, whether comic or deeply hushed, shared by the narrator and Carmen, moments that remind us of the one between his mother and Aston. The poem ends with a nicely apposite turn, by reading the foregoing narrative as integral to the development of the narrator's "conscience", his consciousness of himself as poet, one who "mostly craved / ... the accord of his peers, black or white."

Thompson's gift for the sub-textual is a feature of his work, as in certain other poems about cold, loveless sexual relationships, however intimate. In "Tour of Duty", for example, the context is the US occupation of Japan at the end of the Second World War. The clinical, seemingly distanced recounting of the events of the poem – the "you" of the poem is apparently really the "I" of it – underlines the pain and horror of the humiliation of the vanquished. The layering of ironies complicates the ostensibly matter-of-fact, that-is-the-way the world-is tone, as the poem recalls how the protagonist (the narrator?) enjoyed, as of right, the sordid sweets of conquest. While the central event is the lordly visit of the conquerors to the brothel, and the uneven non-relationship between the officers and the girls, who had "a profitable night", perhaps an even more poignant detail is that the staff car which transports the men to the brothel, prompt to their call, is driven by "a balding ex-professor of History at Tokyo University". Now himself a victim of History, he is "professing" it in a demeaned way – "bowing three times [while] holding the door open."

Each detail in the poem, even the most seemingly casual, works to animate and give concrete immediacy to meaning, as with the "squad of shoes / lined up in the vestibule." Similarly, the "long, straight pins" which Mrs Thwiggs uses to secure her hat image her personality. A feature of Thompson's work is the carefully chosen, carefully placed image, or arrangement of images, to vividly picture, moment, meaning and mood. "Rain Forest House" begins:

> Rain forest house – four thousand feet up
> the mountain in a drizzled valley, the fog
> clutching at our lapels as we push a path
> through tree ferns, vines and bracken
> to a cold clearing, where the house waits
> hugging itself.

And, at "That Time of Day:"

Noon, bloated with heat,
sun-stroked when the village clock bongs twelve.
Shadows hold their breath
waiting to stride out later.
Sheets and towels with pinched nostrils
on clotheslines hang out to dry.
Lizards sleep under rocks…

In "sun-stroked" it is as if the sun is itself a clock striking the heat of midday.

Thompson moves adeptly within a range of familiar forms and styles, from aphoristic brevity and a knowing light-verse lilt to free verse, with, along the way, a characteristic penchant for a relaxed iambic beat and a more or less pentametric line, generally in the direction of blank verse, but sometimes with rhyme, regular or unschematic. In "A Terrible True Tale", the relatively jaunty mix of rhythm and rhyme effectively counterpoints and underlines the horror of the tale, one about how university students catch and, taking the law into their own hands, brutally murder a car thief who has been plaguing their campus.

The poet's attraction to the challenge of strictly disciplined form is evident in his brief forays into haiku and villanelle, and in his rhymed quatrains, as, most impressively, in the sustained technical control of *The View from Mount Diablo*, and now in "The Colour of Conscience". In the latter, the quatrain armature is, as it were, camouflaged, but it is there, holding together the natural-voiced, iambic pentameter flow of the narrative. Of particular note is how the rhyming is sustained, often inventive, without calling attention to itself, and without becoming facile or strained. In their interaction, metre and rhyme work with recurrent enjambement to enhance the narrative flow and voice.

At the end of "The Colour of Conscience", Thompson speaks of "the capriciousness / of death plucking now at [his] octogenarian / beard." The continuing vitality of the Thompson voice is nowhere more evident than in what might be called his octogenarian verse, looking unsentimentally at ageing and death, and with a redeemingly mischievous twinkle in its eye. In "End Game", the eighty-eight-year-old on his deathbed is alive with the raunchiness of senility, imagining his "*ménage a trois* / in Paradise" with his two wives: "Laura with lovely breasts, / Adele the better ass." In the end, though, when his body is wrapped and taken out by the "two attendants from the funeral parlour, soaked in rum," there is no ceremoniousness or piety, no illusion, as they "hefted [him] on their shoulders / down two flights of stairs / to where a rusted pick-up waited."

In "Lift Off," the poet, acknowledging his own infirmities, images himself as on a hurtling, unstoppable jalopy careening downhill:

> Although I have surrendered
> to the discipline of pills,
> doctors' fingers up my arse,
> have swapped cakes and ale
> for oatmeal and Metamucil,
> the downward slope is uncontrollable.

Still, at the last moment, the life spirit in him, as well as something of religious faith in the idea of the other world, makes "the old transport" reverse direction and shoot upward and outward. It is a heady experience: "Curiosity eclipses fear / and who needs bifocals/ for beatific vision?" We are left musing, and amused.

"Hooray for Grey" leaves us with a similarly wry but life-affirming ambiguity. Thompson is a gifted painter in oils, and here, confronting decrepitude and death to affirm what Derek Walcott called the strength of grey ("To Return to the Trees", 1976), he takes us through a palette of colours to look at Albert Huie at the easel, "subdu[ing] a flood / of excess island sunshine with the restraint of umber." The poem ends: "Today, I am in a grey mood, / head in the clouds." The play of meanings here is itself the life of creativity. While "head in the clouds" is a mildly self-deprecating acknowledgement of being fanciful, not keeping one's feet on the ground, it also suggests that the "beatific vision" is the ultimate reality.

NEW POEMS

For Derek Walcott
Friend and Mentor

TAKING WORDS FOR A WALK

Paul Klee, the painter, took a line for a stroll
and I likewise am taking words for a walk.
A dog straining at a leash
of least resistance is towing me
down streets as long as a sentence by Proust,
into an avenue of Kafka ambiguities.

At an intersection two verbs meet,
sniffing each other's tense,
snarling insults at their respective nouns
which are a breed apart –
some short haired, with sharp Anglo-Saxon jaws,
some mellifluously Latinate with long silky ears.

What started as a Sunday stroll
is now a pilgrimage, words with minds of their own
exploring where angels fear to tread,
conservative mastiffs guarding all right turns,
liberal fox terriers yapping at the corners
of lost causes, a cynical mongrel
pausing to baptize a Mercedes with a piddle.

What is sad is when at 3 a.m. in a dream or half sleep
a word warns you of its advent with a low growl
and you know at once it is the key
to the perfection of your poem, but you are too smug
to write it down, thinking you created it
and in the morning it is gone, an empty leash
swinging from the hook behind the door.

RAIN FOREST HOUSE

Rain forest house – four thousand feet up
the mountain in a drizzled valley, the fog
clutching at our lapels as we push a path
through tree ferns, vines and bracken
to a cold clearing where the house waits
hugging itself. My uncle lavishes love
on pale hydrangeas massed like blue brains
over an acre of our reclusive hill.

An aunt, the chatelaine,
keeper of keys to closets, cabinets and
cupboards locked like her virginity,
hums dry tunes, her hands two fluttering birds
afraid to perch, but on morning walks
she harries me to read aloud at each
milepost a chapter of Stevenson or Poe.

Eve to my Adam in this mildewed Eden,
the cook's sixteen-year-old daughter
helps me build a tree house
where she seduces me, the fog twisting itself
around us like a sour blanket.

Some Fridays a friend of my mother
arrives in a Buick, the driver instructed to return on Sunday.
At night, the fire and the kerosene lanterns lit,
the friend lounges in the leather chair,
my mother buffing his nails.
I wind the gramophone – a reedy
aria of love vibrating through the bamboo needle.
"Say good-night," my mother urges;
"it's time for bed."

I am told my father lives in New York
and hope one day to meet him, confident
he will shake my hand and offer me a cigarette.
Now I walk the country roads alone,
head down, kicking stones, the valley
clogged with guilt for what I know
and for what I will never know.

MY UNCLE, THE BISHOP

When news came of his collapse
on the cathedral altar after one of his fiery sermons,
my mother immediately allotted blame
and prayers in the same breath. Candles lit,
the adults congregated to chant the rosary.
Mother ordered me, still in short pants,
to kneel on a rock in the garden,
offering the pain for his recovery.
I managed half an hour and went to bed
bruised but exulting that my agony
and sacrifice had saved his life.
For the funeral she bought
long pants to hide my cuts.

STRAIGHT FROM THE HORSE'S MOUTH

She was sixteen, he seventeen, hot as first love
in pre-pill, colonial times,
and there were horses –
she on a grey mare, he on a chestnut gelding.
Tuesdays they met at Up Park Camp,
on an empty field where British soldiers once played polo,
deserted now, guarded by the Wareika hills.

In the amber light of late afternoons
they talked while the horses tossed
their manes and farted.

Her mare half circled left, half circled right,
sometimes a full pirouette,
muscling to the gelding who ignored her.
She wore jodhpurs and a silk blouse,
the top two buttons open, a proper forward seat,
pelvic bone braced to pommel, her body
an exclamation mark. He was
more a question mark, slumped
on the cantle of the saddle,
khaki pants tucked into riding boots,
trying to woo her with mordant wit.

Once she had to pee, dismounted
and, unembarrassed, pulled down her britches
behind the polo stand while he held the horses
trying to look the other way.
There were other limping intimacies
but he remembered best that afternoon she screamed
"Ready!" and lashed the mare into a gallop.
The gelding, outraged at the challenge,
nostrils bellicose, slammed angry hooves into the ground

for traction, but the mare won by a head.
Thereafter, the weekly gallop
became a ritual, ending when he left
for college in America. She still rode every Tuesday
alone on the green plateau
under the protection of the hills,
missing the smell of his sweat, the lather of his horse
until one afternoon, out of the slanting shadows,
a figure rode towards her from the horizon.
She thought it might be him returned, but this rider
was older, taller, darker, mounted on a black stallion.
He straight away challenged her to a gallop
and won by a full length. They agreed
to meet again the following Tuesday……

THE ICE CREAM BUCKET

I recall the clean dirt
of a Jamaican back-yard compacted
by the bare soles of black servants
and the shod feet of white children
in their care, while the people of the house
live their pendulum lives wambling
between sin and repentance.

Bruegel would have envied it:
the curtilage fringed with the green Afros
of *Lignum vitae* trees dense with yellow butterflies
ignorant of their destiny with death,
enjoying the last moments of their passion.
In three tight circles, scouting a resting place,
Rufus, the yard mongrel, settles on his side
in shade, a desultory thump of tail
when the cook's daughter giggles his name,
she just back from church, still in pink
organdy dress and white ankle socks.

Over an open fire "mannish water" bubbles
in a Shell kerosene tin, a languid Sunday breeze
flirting with the smoke. The muscled gardener,
Emperor of Ice Cream, steadies on the top step
a bucket, barrel-staved and paddle-fitted,
the inside wall packed with cracked ice sprinkled
with coarse salt. He needs two hands
to crank the handle, the aroma of vanilla
seeping from the slurry. The paddle
lifted out, the cream begins to drip
and, permission granted, the licking starts –
concupiscence flaring. I hope
my appetite for ice cream will not dwindle
in the after-life, and I am comforted.

SEASONS

After a hard winter
Spring wafts in the window
smelling of thawed soil and cut grass.
Thus *langueur* begins,
(I am studying French in a strange land
quartered by seasons),
mope and nope caught up in my reveries
stalling the affairs of men.

I imagine a young girl skipping rope,
levitating at the apogee of jump,
floating off into a Chagall painting:
a conquistador parks his pike in a corner,
mumbling mañana, and Vivaldi,
after a night's adventure, knows the score
but will not lift a fist to note
a minim or a quaver... later... later.

I look through the open window
and even in the torpor of this interregnum
I can see in my village
bougainvillea bursting into bloom,
the frank tumescence of anthurium lilies,
the whole seething, teeming, heaving,
jig, jiggle, jerk and jolt of year-round germination,
a pregnant girl sashaying confidently by,
a summer in her step, a belly full of hope.
The French language, I have learned,
has no single word for what I mean by homesickness.
J'ai le mal du pays!
Lord, how I miss my island.

LEAF RAKER

I look at an old man sweeping leaves
into little piles along a row
of almond trees that line the sidewalk,
his rake sometimes at shoulder arms
to let a group of early morning workers through,
their eyes averted from his smouldering gaze.

I invent for him a history
he can't refute: steep rise
to wattle shack and hillside field
where he has planted yams, dammed
a pool for ducks, even rooted out
the paw paw tree she claimed had tamed
his nature. She left him anyway,
and his mind, jolted to a halt between
revenge and resignation, commanded him
to come to town where, if he swept
the sidewalks clean, one day he might see her strolling by.

I surmise that in the curve of each pink leaf
he sees the linger of her lips
or in the crackle underfoot
hears her hectoring voice.
As if impatient with this fiction, a morning breeze
chops the harbour into waves, swirls
up the street dishevelling the almond trees,
banging my window shut,
ending the story. But a truth abides – the rake
scraping its teeth over hard ground
into a litter of stirring leaves – for love's sake,
an old man at his task defying the wind.

TRUTH AND CONSEQUENCES

They were a close family
but with space enough between the loving
for everyone to grow.
At four the son asked,
"Who made God?" and the father,
building a steeple with his fingers,
declared, "God made God!"
The oracle had spoken and truth
seemed suddenly as clear
as switching on the kitchen light.

At seven doctors discovered
a hole in his heart. Surgery was scheduled
and he asked, "Will I die?"
"I don't think so," his mother replied,
"but all life is in God's hands."
When he awoke, father on one side,
mother on the other, his birthday watch
still ticking, belief blazed
like the overhead light
in the operating room before he fell asleep.

At ten, dimpled, with soft brown eyes,
a coterie of nubile girls pursued him daily
and another puzzle nagged at him,
a word of one syllable
with the barking sound of "K".
So he asked his grandmother
in a guiltless voice, "Is cunt
the worst of all bad words?"
Her poise rattled, she recovered
sufficiently to mumble, "Not particularly
apt for church or school", and his father

explained it was a medical term
in many Eighteenth Century texts,
an inner point from which to measure
and affirm the address of other organs.
Once more the oracles had spoken.

And then came love...
a girl's embracing arms,
a shimmering shawl of well being.
He consulted his parents
who tossed him between *Eros* and *Agape*,
finally admitting that love was a mystery
only he could solve.

REGRET

We were lovers once who tried
Perhaps too hard.
Now the past has slipped
Like an embarrassed smile
Into memory's abyss and you know, beloved,
Abyss is as good as a mile

FEATURE

A village hall with a tin roof named *Cinema Royal*
where for a shilling on a Saturday night the folk,
mostly men, flocked to see a thriller or a cowboy flick.

A single projector eyeballs the sheet stretched
as a screen, flickering to a stop when the first reel ends
just as the Indians are circling the wagons.
In the second act, unloaded from its canister,
Tom Mix rides to the rescue.

When a Hitchcock thriller is the feature
the silence of suspense as the murderer
stalks the unsuspecting victim is unbearable.
For relief a voice bellows "Puss"
and melodrama unravels into laughter.

When John Wayne and Gary Cooper mix it up
in a fist fight to the death, the lads jump from their seats,
mimicking in the aisle the action on the screen,
shouting "Lick him down!", an enthusiast enacting
an uppercut that spins him round.

Chairs knocked over,
as the on-and-off-screen battle rages
until the theatre owner sitting in the back row
flips a switch beside him,
and a sign at the bottom of the screen lights up.

"Shut up and sit down
or there will be no more movie tonight";
it flashes two or three times as the patrons
reluctantly return to their seats
just as Wayne knocks Cooper down and wins the fight.

The owner's total take is sixty shillings,
less than the cost to rent the film.
Yet those days were rich in peace,
catharsis stored in tin cans for another showing.

THAT TIME OF DAY

Noon, bloated with heat,
sun-stroked when the village clock bongs twelve.
Shadows hold their breath,
waiting to stride out later.
Sheets and towels with pinched nostrils
on clotheslines hang out to dry.
Lizards sleep under rocks;
the wind has a hint of scorch,
as if about to catch fire.
The asphalt of main street bubbles
and the branches of palms
hang down unsapped.

But all is not lost.
In the tropics there is always
an oasis of cool –
under the long body of a parked truck,
under the thatch of a lean-to,
or the shade of a Panama hat.

Dogs find shelter like a buried bone,
their bellies on damp earth.
The silence of noon
is loud, a conserving of energy
for the afternoon awakening
when shadows leap out of hiding.
Washing is plucked into baskets,
lizards thresh through the undergrowth,
asphalt hardens back to a road
and the branches of trees lift up in alleluias.

WEDDING FLOWERS

I who have no skill with bloom or leaf
watch ladies fixing flowers for a wedding
on the Cafe Caribe's floating dock
where the bride and her attendants will disembark
from a rented glass-bottom boat, newly repainted,
festooned with purple bunting, burnished
with cocoa leaves spray-painted gold. There,
under a swaying bamboo arch, the bride will
tomorrow marry Tony, Lieutenant Colonel,
Jamaica Defence Force Reserves,
in civilian life a junior cost accountant.

I am surrounded by an infinite array
of flora bunched in basins, ewers, pans –
reservoirs to capture beauty's overflowing:
white arum lilies lifted from a bucket, dandled
like a baby on a young girl's breast;
huge breadfruit leaves Egyptian handmaidens
might have waved to cool an over-ardent queen.
For one brilliant hour I have been high
on flowers. But they are gone now.
A lizard slithers across the tiles,
surrendering the shadows to a milking asp.

HOORAY FOR GREY

I keep in memory the flamboyant colours
that excited and consoled my sunlit youth,
a battery of brightness so intense the flowers
bombarded my sight even with my eyes closed.
Now, with age, I prefer the subtle harmonies
of greys, complementaries I arrange on a palette
in my mind – the viridian green of forest leaves
mixed in equal measure with the alizarin of bougainvilleas,
this concoction cut with the titanium white
of daisies to offer up a range of shades
and temperatures. For the cold gunmetal bite
of a rifle barrel add to the grey mix
a dab of cobalt blue and feel the weapon
freeze your fingers to the trigger. For the warmth
of a bed sheet in a sunny room depend upon
some yellow ochre brushed into the blend
to glow the canvas hotter. A week ago
I watched Whistler paint his mother's shawl.
Yesterday I visited Huie's Cross Roads studio
where Albert at his oils studiously subdued a flood
of excess island sunshine with the restraint of umber.
And today? Today I am in a grey mood,
head in the clouds.

BOSTON BAY

At Boston Bay one moonlight night,
our clothes in piles upon the sand,
we prowed our bodies through the waves
and Brailled each other's nakedness.
This love, my love, will warm our memories.
Even Lazarus between the sores
and dog licks recalled the sheen of skin,
the swell of breast, the sanctuaries of flesh
when God was resting from his work.
No need to lift this Lazarus up.
Before the blight there will be time
to race again to Boston Bay,
to catch the moon before it wanes
and scrawl our names across the sand.

OLDER AT TERRA NOVA HOTEL

Here is a rhyme
that winds down fast
now that my batteries are weak.
I danced with the ladies on this floor,
cheek to cheek,
and more to more,
from time to time
in ages past
and oh the memories are sweet.

AUBADE

He awakes the following day,
The remembered scent of kisses sweetening
His early morning breath,
His early morning thoughts
Nudging the memory of his delicious sin,
Unperturbed by whether it is due to passion
Or simply an excess of gin.

He casts aside the sheets
As well as any lingering doubts,
Smiles a sincere if silent greeting
To his still sleeping wife,
Heads for the shower
And turns his face like a child
About to utter an impertinence
Up to the spray. With water trickling
Down his chest and groin he begins to pray.

"I am grateful for this new *if.*
Let it be crisp as laundered linen,
Cool as the passion in a fencer's foil."
Then winceing at the thought
And because the water is too hot
He castigates himself for dreaming utter rot.
Yet there remains a sweet constriction
In his throat and against his fingers,
The bird flutter of a lingering hope.
He cannot bring himself to let it go
So he shuts his mind instead
Watching the water at his feet
Chase itself in circles down the drain.

VIEWPOINT

It's right to honour houses that command a view,
An embrace of distant prospects delighted in.
A foreground needs horizons for vistas to accrue.

A box with squinting windows will not do.
We need verandahs above the city's din.
It's right to honour houses that command a view.

Spy from your perch a bird's impromptu slew,
Look down on neighbours but without a trace of sin.
A foreground needs horizons for vistas to accrue.

A point of view, unchallenged, must be true,
Dogmatic perhaps like preaching ancient doctrine.
It's right to honour houses that command a view.

The world needs more pandiculation in lieu
Of dinge, outsightfulness where dark has been.
A foreground needs horizons for vistas to accrue.

Altitude brings cooling breezes too,
Bestowing blessings on priest and Philistine.
It is right to honour houses that command a view.
A foreground needs horizons for vistas to accrue.

TALBOT THWIGGS

(for Louis Simpson)

Talbot Thwiggs
in the seventy-third year of his life,
the forty-fifth of his marriage,
turns to his wife who is dressing
for Sunday service and says,
"I want to buy a dog."

"What on earth for?" she asks,
adjusting her hat in the mirror
with long, straight pins.

"I dunno. Dogs romp, wag
their tails when you talk to them,
kiss your hands, your face."

"I never heard such nonsense,"
she exclaims. "Hurry up
or we'll be late for church."

LADY IN A BLACK HALF-SLIP

A lady in a black half-slip
pirouettes before a mirror
proud of her discrepancies –
the jot of one nipple
unequal to the tittle of its twin,
arch of one eyebrow
flatter than the other,
the left corner of her mouth
higher than the right.
She is happy for her lovers to discover
her assault on symmetry.
Deserter from the dominion
of the straight and narrow,
she awaits a date to celebrate
her history, descending now
the spiral staircase to the kitchen
where she mixes a martini
carried in both hands like a chalice
to greet the man who rings
her doorbell, confident her half-slip
defines her nakedness, but not all of her.

TOUR OF DUTY

Japan was occupied territory then,
land of the setting sun.
A Flying Tiger transport touches down
at Haneda Air Force base:
a new contingent of the conquerors
disembarking in rumpled uniforms.

Your true status is confirmed
when after two weeks on station
and after two martinis at the officers' club
you phone the motor pool
and in five minutes a staff car arrives
(always a basic blue Chevrolet), the driver
a balding ex-professor of History at Tokyo University,
bowing three times, holding the door open.

The entrance to the house is hung
with ferns, water from a bamboo gutter
cooling the stone steps, a squad of shoes
lined up in the vestibule. It will be a profitable night
for the girls. The room is a warm amber glow
to match the pale yellow soles of tiny feet
reflected from the tatami mats.

And when you zipper up,
there is the professor bowing again
and you are driven sedately back to base
like an ambassador who has just presented
his credentials at the Imperial Palace.

SAME OLD STORY

"All politics is local,"
Proclaim the pundits.
And old poets know
Myths begin as rumour,
All epics start with
"Once upon a time."

PROPHECY

Try it! Plant your feet
on level ground under
an early morning moon.
Then take the measure of yourself
from toe tip to scalp,
estimating how many intervals
of your height would close the gap
between you and the moon.

Aiming straight up,
my average count is fifteen,
twenty to be safe.
Suppose you reckon thirty,
would it defy belief
that you could climb a rope
let down from above?
I grant it must be strong,
long-fibred flax perhaps,
or sisal, thick as a snake
where you would grab it,
narrowing to a thin thread
at the higher end,
bellying slightly from the line of sight,
linking your eye to whoever
steadies it above.

Of course, there should be knots,
spaced evenly in the rope
to offer purchase for your toes,
a halt to catch your breath
before the next ascent.
Half way up, your courage
will be tested not to look
back at our beloved earth.

How long it will take to reach
the top I cannot say
but I need no scattering of bones,
no eagle's entrails, to prophesy
that a man like us one day
will shinny to the moon.

ALARUM

This is a strange mid-morning storm, tropical, intense,
the gods pissing down rain to dampen the fever of commerce
in an exclusive banking cul-de-sac where cars are parked in ranks
on both sides of the street, alarms set, grills sneering
defiance at passersby. Things are hotting up above,
minor deities flinging lightning like frisbees across the sky.

Then the big boss booms a thunder bolt, one almighty clap
that triggers all the car alarms – a dissonance of pulsing
squawks, skirls, barking horns and blinking lights, chassis
shaking on their springs, expecting the second coming of Christ.
But He is only passing through, His bastinado echoing now
to silence in the surrounding hills, the cars sheepishly
resetting their alarms

CONSTRUCTION

They say Native Ameri-
cans have no fear of
heights so after a day of
bolting steel I am resting
on my back twenty sto-
reys up the steel skeleton
of this skyscraper,
stretched out on a cold
I-beam twelve inches
wide, one hand across
my chest, the other dan-
gling down, the tips of
my fingers two hundred
feet above the ground.
Now that you share this
altitude with me do your
fingers tingle like mine?
It is up to you either to
leave me balanced here
until first light or before
the sun sets and the lights
below begin to beckon,
you can will me to stand
up, arms outstretched,
teetering to safety across
the beam. One way or
the other only you can
bring this poem to an
end

CONSTRICTION

My orifice of love
is not an infinity of roundness
through which could pass
a caravan of camels.
It is rather a pin-prick in a cardboard sheet,
no enlargement possible
except under a magnifying glass.

Constriction is hereditary,
as tight as the fist that gripped
my mother's throat and strangled
her inside out, or as myopic
as my father's aspic gaze
behind his rimless glasses.
But even a slit held up to just one eye
can frame the universe.

On extraordinary days I have awakened
confirmed in my belief that roses
bloom outside the window, holding
their breath for the arrival of the hyacinth girl.
On a high hill's brink guarding this garden,
I verge on great discoveries and with arms
outstretched like wings happily fling
myself into uncertainties.
But a fit of logic breaks my fall.
I erupt in syllogisms
hived with categorical imperatives,
and this rash behaviour drives me sane.

SEARCH

Time to twirl the dial of the combination lock.
Click! The steel door swings open. In the dark
your fingers fumble for the switch to light a bulb,
the symbol of enlightenment if only you can turn it on.
In the damp humidity of the vault's interior,
ideas bubble, waiting to drip from the edge of a shelf.
You grope through memory's memorabilia –
a rosary, a rusty military medal, a cancelled promissory note –
and withdraw empty minded.
But there have been surprises – the unexpected
plush of a hinged box, its silk lining
caressing a small pearl, glowing, unafraid
of the dark, waiting to be strung into a necklace
like the right order of words.

THE LUNATIC

A committed artist, he lived
contentedly in the asylum
until one day he jumps up
on a table in the cafeteria
proclaiming his disenchantment
with perspective. While the warden
listens, he insists he can compress
the world into a wafer disk
for better communion with his fellow sinners.
He raises a fist, proclaiming
he will upend the horizon
and the table top on which he stands.
If only things were thin,
razor blades would substitute for rocks
in all his landscapes, advancing composition
to the cutting edge of art.

How wonderful to abolish roundness,
to pare down the flanks of mountains
and squeeze the redundant sap from trees.
Perspective is a trick practised
by prison guards marching inmates
between receding railway tracks
until they disappear forever at the vanishing point.
"I am ready to attack all jutting, rounded things,
foreshortened jetties, pointed fingers,
bosoms, buttocks, balloons and balls.
Look! I am a pure rectangle,
a golden gate which casts no shadow
through which, in triumph, I will lead the people
into a fifth dimension."
The warden signals and a white-coated paramedic
advances. The ranting stops.

THE EMPEROR OF POSSIBILITIES

His innocence was a silver bell
gracefully curved and burnished,
the singing of its tongue
ringing fainter as he entered deeper
into the Kingdom of Evil –
a forest of effulgent green
teeming with the possibilities of sin,
a royal maze he thought an Emperor could master.
When he had passed
through the thick and thin of it,
arrived at the forest's outer rim
he sat on a rock, hearing the silver anthem
of the bell still faintly ringing in the distance,
remembering that when he was innocent
he could conjecture, tease out
the possibilities of evil but, sated now in sin,
innocence could never be restored –
now no turning back,
not even for an Emperor.

SOME OTHER THINGS THAT GO BUMP IN THE NIGHT

What woke me up, alone
in the dark house, I am not sure –
perhaps a breeze blowing a window open
to let a prayer drift in, or conscience out,
God sighing his mercies, the devil belching.

Something had surely changed,
the floorboards creaking under a heavy boot.
From the study, an old typewriter
suddenly clatters to life, a ghost poet perhaps
recruited to craft my epitaph.

Or was it something more epical –
a lunar eclipse the astronomers had missed,
a slight star-shift sabotaging my horoscope,
prophesying a bad end?

All night my skin crawls
as the gale rattles the windows.
But the shadows retreat before the sun,
hiding under my bed,
and hope is the palaver
of early morning birds.

FINAL FLIGHT

There it is, the Concorde,
still a silver elegance, its swordfish bill
strapped now to the deck
of an oily brown barge ploughing
slowly through dense water
to be baptized a dockside museum
where tourists, five quid a pop,
will queue, pawing through
passenger lists to find the seat
that cushioned Elizabeth Taylor's ass.

But Orville's ghost, still sniffing
the possibilities of lift for this
unblemished craft, sun glinting
from his aviator glasses, floats
into the cockpit and Concorde soars
once more, no sound, just two gloved hands
pushing gently forward on the throttle.

SEA ANEMONES

Philemon and Baucis Jones,
married fifty years to the day,
boarded their flight from New York
to Paris, happy to have booked first class.

When the nose of the plane blew off,
the fractured frame lifted
for one improbable moment, nothing
between their bulkhead seats
and the early evening stars flinching
at this heretical manoeuvre.

They knew, of course, it was only
a matter of time,
having practiced for so long
how to reckon it, contented now
to cease the counting.

"Sea Anemones," he whispered in her ear
as the ocean opened to receive them.

ON THE RETIREMENT OF AN AIRLINE PILOT

We are the membership of the amazed
that someone essentially as frail
as us, flesh and blood, of average build,
can urge earth-hugging steel to sail

through air and, at the dally of fingertips
on dials, to lift, bank and climb
out of the common sense of gravity
into a new geography that compresses time.

Now down to earth from one last flight
after thirty years of racing with the sun
we step from the cockpit onto *terra firma*
happy to be back where we'd begun.

FIRST A GREEN LEAF

Through a crack in the wall,
first a green leaf,
then a lily pushes
and suddenly the room
is full of flowers
in so many shapes and scents
he knows his mind
is playing tricks again.

He keeps his eyes shut
and the flowers begin to fade
into a kaleidoscope
of lights, purple shading
into green, a red dot
pulsing at the centre
of the screen behind his eyes.

He is an auditorium of one
waiting to clap the performance,
to shout *Bravo.* But there will be
no encores tonight. Time
to tear up the theatre stub,
to shrug on coat
and start the return journey
to wherever sights and smells
are stored, to where
on a table there is a glass
of water beside a tray of pills.

ELEGY FOR MY FATHER

Old age gripped him,
first by the ankles,
and when it worked its way
up to his knees
the doctors diagnosed Parkinson's.

Our house was raucous
with growing kids
and it seemed unfair
to drown him in their laughter
or to whisper them silent
in the eddies of his pain.
So we built a cottage on the compound,
detached in a sense
but close enough if not for love
certainly for respect.

One day he fell and broke his hip.
His private room at the hospital
opened onto a verandah
and a wild garden bursting
with cocoa leaves and ginger lilies.

When he slipped from pneumonia
into a coma we sat for hours, days,
on the verandah listening to him
trying to link words together –
sometimes the word "war"
(he had been a soldier)
sometimes "No, no. Please."

On the third morning of the vigil
I turned to my wife. “Everything is so quiet.
I can hear the pigeons lifting from the roof,
the lizards thrashing through the grass.”
She reached over and held my hand.

THE DAY MAY COME

The day may come, my love,
when some passing cold cloud
will dim your eyes, casting a shadow
on your smile fighting its own diminishing,
and I will stand beside the bed,
touching my knuckles to your cheek,
incapable of more than that profound
but feeble ministration
for which you will be beholden.
And I will grieve a little less
seeing in your eyes
not only pain but past reflections
when at another time and place
I overshadowed you.

I HAVE NOT SCORNED MY LIFE

Nor have I savoured it;
no warm remembrances
of a sailor who can recall
the seasons, who harbours
in his memory each port
that gave him anchorage.
In the cove of my heart
the waves are always restless,
fitful eddies breaking on the beach.
I have had the time of my life
and like a spendthrift frittered it away.

ELEGY

That time-worn cliché death
has rhymed him out at last, stiff
as a sonnet, the priest chanting a wreath
of words around his coffin,
the sanctuary light still beckoning,
frantic with hope. Only his poems remain,
awkward as shovelled gravel,
to pitch his voice beyond the grave.

DEATH WISH

When it is my time
to die I wish to lift off from my sick bed
floating
up to heaven like a Chagall angel
in a ballooning nightdress
sans underwear, an updraft
tickling my testicles,
up, up and away,

below the loved ones
waving good-bye
growing smaller and smaller and smaller

HAIKU VARIATIONS

Spring Rain

Drizzle dimples the pool.
Eaves drip. Then comes
The jubilation of frogs.

Jamaican Summer

Dogs crawl under trucks for shade.
Fridges struggle
To make lukecool water.

Fall

Adam and Eve try sin.
Their blushes tint
The leaves of the garden red.

STRATEGIES

I'd rather ask forgiveness than seek permission,
the bureaucracy of begging takes too long.
Whatever is worth the doing validates the mission.

In courting girls I learned in intermission
the urge to overcome reluctance must be strong;
I'd rather ask forgiveness than seek permission.

My lover's father, opposed to my religion,
refused her hand in marriage which I thought was wrong.
Whatever is worth the doing validates the mission.

We eloped, drugged by a romantic vision
till the funds ran out – an old dilemma's prong.
I'd rather ask forgiveness than seek permission.

I then divorced her, the cost a bitter lesson,
but rewon freedom was a new enchanting song.
Whatever is worth the doing validates the mission.

Satan takes advantage of a mere suspicion
of libido, ready to beat his welcoming gong.
I'd rather ask forgiveness than seek permission.
Whatever is worth the doing validates the mission.

INTRODUCTION TO A BOOK OF PHOTOGRAPHS

A photographer, seeing eye to eye
with the camera, crouches
behind a tripod waiting for a bough
to sway, a cloud to pass,
an inner voice to whisper *now,*
then clicks a book of photographs to life
and I, flipping the images,
hold an island in my hand.

Here is a contest between the tropical lush
of landscape and the camera's black and white
austerities. A mountain range
climbing across a page is dimmed
behind the scrim of a fisherman's net
cast high from a canoe anchored in the bay.

In late afternoon light
three boys, black drovers,
drive a line of Biblical sheep
into a dappled forest straddling
two middle pages of the book.

Every artist knows how to separate
sheep from goats, this goat
perched on the pediment
of a wall three stories high
in a deserted village, no evidence
of how ascent was possible
unless the camera beamed him up.

Two lizards kiss. A standpipe drips
a single tear. The goat god stands
patiently on guard
as shutter and sun fight
for the hegemony of light.

BROOM MAN

I wake from a Saturday jag
to a voice booming, "Brooms! Brooms!
Get your cobweb broom!" –
the broom man trudging barefoot
through upper residential streets,
his cargo slung over a shoulder,
a Kotex pad stuffed under the load
to comfort a blister –
the limit of technology he can muster
but still embarrassed to buy
the woman box in public.

He has cut saplings in eight-foot lengths,
threads and plaits dried palm fronds
into a chignon at the broom's base,
the foliage flaring into a yellow skirt.
He has no lathe to round the handles,
just the sandpaper smudge
of a black hand signing its art.

The next door neighbour offers water
in a tin cup (no glass to disinfect).
When he knocks at my gate I ask him in.
We sit on the garden wall and chat,
stalemated between prejudice and pride
and since there is nothing to lose or gain
I share with him the work
of crafting poems and in exchange
he sweeps away the cobwebs from my brain.

PRIDE AND PREJUDICE

He arrived in the island from Minnesota
with an MA degree in English
and a fine curiosity about black culture.
After six months he married a black woman
to discover for himself
how she might be different from a white woman
about things that really mattered –
like love, courage, destiny, death.

When it was clear there were no differences,
the marriage ended abruptly.
She was just another woman –
vulnerable, honest, unpredictable,
passionate, intelligent, confused,
cunning, repentant. She understood Dante,
Walcott and Soyinka, debated Sylvia Plath,
puzzled at St. John of the Cross,
challenged cross-word puzzles,
had difficulty calculating percentages.

As a minor poet he knew he could find
no objective correlative
for such a state of affairs.
Only then did he notice her different body odour,
the yellow bottoms of her feet,
her yellow palms, the blue-grey of her nipples,
the absolute absence of pink even in her gums.

On his return to Minnesota
he told his friends she had left him
for a black man better hung.
And they believed him.

RED BIRD

A red bird flew in the window,
clamped a calloused claw
around my index finger.
Obviously not a raven,
I wondered at the reason
for this crimson visitation.

Slowly I raised my hand
to test if we could see eye to eye
on what it meant. It took
two of mine to one of his
and he did not blink.

I could not out-stare him,
my scrutiny bent back
in the mirror of his gaze,
set in a band of green
which made his red feathers blaze.

Thus inflamed, I half expected him
to flourish out of his throat
some message from the sacred wood,
at least one brief note
of explanation, but he remained unruffled.

I backed away from the encounter
and as I dropped my hand
he flipped his tail, splattered
a blessing in my lap and lifted off,
the broken edges of bewildered air
closing around the red blur of his departure.

ROOTS

The switch of choice
is thin and supple,
welts festering in the boy's black skin,
one for each year of his defiance,
fingers practicing in secret to curl
around the barrel of an AK-47.
The teachers cut their switches
from the tamarind tree which spreads
a fine shade across the school yard.
Under his bare feet
he can feel the roots growing
wide as the branches,
plotting underground to crack
the foundations of the school house walls,
to burst the pediments,
to snap the roof's spine.

A BRIEF BIOGRAPHY

Teacher and student conjugate
a verbal brawl which escalates
to insults. The boy,
with no inventory of words,
cannot match the teacher's vituperation
so he snatches an ice pick from his waist
and plunges it into her ear.

The teacher collapses, the boy
runs to his mother who hides him.
He does not know his father
who vanished before his birth.
At night he slinks into the shadows
where a Don dispenses favours.
In thanksgiving for a Taurus automatic
the boy pledges an allegiance which swells
his depleted manhood.

He sells drugs. His mother yearns
to turn him over to the police, the only way
to save his life, but knows one of his cronies
will kill her as an informer.
Alone, smoking a spliff,
he sees through the cloud of smoke
the teacher's face in profile, silent words
shooting from her lips like a stream
of fire from a flame thrower.

A TERRIBLE TRUE TALE

The hot-wire genius takes set on the college,
interested more in loot than in knowledge.
Students are losing their cars at night,
each theft invigorating his appetite.

Ten cars vanish in thirty days.
The owners, frustrated at official delays
and bumbling bureaucratic excuses, set
their own trap for the thief – a quartet

of sentries assigned to each car with cell phones,
flashlights and petrol. In one of the watch zones
a figure is spotted crouched in the grass,
alerting the students who assemble *en masse*,

storming from dorms in bellicose groups.
Beams from their torches swirl in loops
across the campus, a circle of light
growing smaller and tighter, the prey in their sight.

Disoriented and winded, he heads
For a gate, stumbles into a cesspool instead.
Before he can cling to the edge, the stoning
and jeering commence, no time for atoning.

He flays in the fusion of urine and faeces
overpowered by the stench the mixture releases.
They stamp in the tall dry grass and taunt him
igniting with gas a circle of fire, the dim

dawn now tinged in orange flame.
"Help me," he screams, "in Jesus' name!"
Unable to swim, he stirs up the mire,
the level of crud reaching higher and higher.

A student leader breaks through the smoke,
kneels, eye-balls him and with one stroke
boxes away a hand he had raised
in supplication. Unfeeling, unfazed,

she sings, "It's time you understand,
our generation will lead this land
and we are firm in our belief:
death too good for motor car thief."

Kissing her teeth the smoke lady retreats,
her song now a chorus by the other elites.
Brigade and cop cars scream in the distance,
the mob leader commanding, "Show no resistance.

We disclaim any blame for the pre-dawn grass burn,
return of the vehicles our only concern."
Blood lust now a diluted red,
they focus their hunger on breakfast instead.

The police find him face down in the pit,
lifeless arms embracing its shit.
The Superintendent holds his nose.
"He got what he deserved, I have to suppose."

Later, the students assemble for prayers
and to sing the National Anthem, (theirs
is a Christian college, at least in name).
Solemn sounds rising from whence they came

soulful with feeling. *Eternal Father*
Bless our land, the words drifting higher,
the chorus ascending on a breeze from the hills
as the emptied cesspool slowly refills.

VALLEY OF DECISION

The valley fills to the brim
with slanting light spilling
from the hills as the gold clock-face
of the sun winds down for the day,
the gentle pastoral scarred
by a boy in a black coat,
a bomb strapped to his back.
He and his love slog up a stream,
before them Ramallah and corpses
wrapped in flags waiting
to be lowered into earth not yet a nation.
Miriam had beseeched him not to leave her
and offers one virgin in the flesh
for the seventy-two in Paradise promised to martyrs.
A virgin himself, he feels the itch of the bomb
in the small of his back, on his chest
the soft imprint of her breasts.
He cups water from the stream
to relieve his thirst for justice and gently fingers
the detonation device – the die long since cast.

RECOVERY

Wind flings a fist into the window pane
spreading a coverlet of glass over the bed.
Trees, rocked to their roots, topple
sideways in a sigh of leaves. Roofs lift.
Shingles and zinc sheets zig-zag overhead
like kites. Gullies overflow,
swirl the city's garbage to the sea –
plastic bags, an amputated chair,
the carcass of a dog with stiff outstretched paws…

When it is over the storm has drawn
a new perspective in its wake, old landmarks
vanished, structures once obscured
by trees and shacks now given pride of place,
a new bird's eye-view of the drenched land.

But this is generous ground. Already
a deal for new growth has been struck
with the sun. A jolt of germination
begins to thrum in the groin of the earth,
the wind-flayed skeleton of a poinciana tree
suddenly crowned in orange flames.

NOEL

There is something that might be said,
some exclamation tangled in the brain
leaving a shred behind, not lost
exactly but muffled on the tongue,
some note of exultation waiting to be sung.
Or perhaps there is something on the verge
of vision, a mood of expectation
no more ponderous than the precise twist
of an infant's wrist responding
to the patient coaching of a parent,
a galaxy of small bones circling a blessing.
A beginning. Time too new
to be defined, too fresh to be defiled.
How can such a tiny God
bestow free will, imposing on himself
the burden of foreknowledge?

LESSONS

Before he became a preacher
he had to be a learner,
how to smile, how a sphincter
muscle worked, his mother splashing water
between his legs from a pitcher
to clean him up. Older,
he loved to watch his father
bent over a piece of dry lumber
from Lebanon, organizing the inner
workings of the plane, a chuck tapped closer
to the blade, locking it in place, a slither
of skin peeling from the wood, his fingers
reeking with the smell of cedar. A quick learner,
but at the next lesson a shudder
shook his body as the carpenter
crossed two planks, offering him nails and hammer
to fix the junction of a cross. This was harder
than preaching in the temple, no matter
how he tried to master
the hang of it.

BROWN SUGAR

Washed in a beatitude of island light,
a grey-haired couple lunch in a white gazebo
perched on the brink of a brick patio
at the edge of a private sea, a butler
serving garnished sandwiches and grapes.
He bows, then fades into the purple shadows of the villa –
the beach, the bay, the reef,
composing prospects for a new millennium.

Adulteries confessed, forgiven and forgotten
in the long, languid postcoital slumber of a century's passing,
they sit in silence sipping coffee from terra cotta mugs,
hearing the steady roll-call of an ocean
oblivious to time other than its own reckoning of tides.

A venerable palm, short on sap,
tinges to yellow, trying not to lean.
A cloud blurs a corner of the blue sky
warning of rain. Time to go.
They drain their cups, the sweet silt
of brown sugar lingering on their lips.

END GAME

Lifted to the light
the x-ray of his liver crackled,
speckled with random dots,
as if the film was past its expiry date.
But at 88 he understood
death was overdue. He wrote
a will and took to bed in silk pajamas,
attended by Adele, his second wife –
Laura, his first, two decades dead,
presumably in heaven.
A priest practiced in consolations
dipped a finger into holy oil and crossed
his forehead, certifying resurrection of the body.

"When Adele dies," the old man mused,
"I will be the third of a *menage a trois*
in Paradise, Laura with lovely breasts,
Adele the better ass. Perhaps, after all,
time is just a waste of eternity."

Flesh kept melting from his bones.
Then one evening Adele collapsed in the courtyard
crying, "He's gone! He's gone!
He held my hand and whispered, 'I love you,
Laura.' The wrong wife for God's sake!"

Two attendants from the funeral parlour, soaked with rum,
surfeited with death, shirts open to the waist,
wrapped him in a sheet tied with twine
at ankle, waist and chin, a white worm
hefted on their shoulders
down two flights of stairs
to where a rusted pick-up waited.

LIFT OFF

(For Edward Baugh)

Well, here I am, obliged to steer
the octogenarian jalopy rattling
down the steep incline of the last lap,
tyres bald, headlights dim, brakes
unresponsive to my pumping.

Although I have surrendered
to the discipline of pills,
doctors' fingers up my arse,
have swapped cakes and ale
for oatmeal and Metamucil,
the downward slope is uncontrollable.

I cherish the brief distraction
of the landscape speeding by,
the blur of green trees
against a blue Madonna sky,
muscled mountains guarding the city,
bougainvillea waving their ebullient farewells.
I am reconciled, I think, to the final splash
into the calm Sargasso at road's end.

But just in time the old transport
lifts off like a spaceship sailing
silently away from earth,
the redundant steering wheel
spinning aimlessly. A star
flares the start of a new voyage.
Curiosity eclipses fear
and who needs bifocals
for beatific vision?

ESPOUSALS

(For John Figueroa)

After the dregs of racial pride
There is humanity.
After the ashes of patriotism
There is brotherhood.
After the dogmas of religion
There is conscience.
After the ullage of ideology
There is common sense.
After the echo of poetry
There is poetry

IT'S A DEAL

Grow old along with me!
The best is yet to be
– Robert Browning

Now by His grace I have outlived my penis
and this brings a peace of sorts. But how to cope
with memory, its walls scrawled with graffiti
of recall, where itch still lingers dreaming
ecstasies of scratch. But I have learned
from Job to bargain with a God – a deal
that He, post mortem, will contra the excruciations
of my journey against the penances
assigned to sin, the divine books balanced.
Before Alzheimer's dirty sleeve erases all,
quick, write a poem.

THE COLOUR OF CONSCIENCE

"*Only those can understand us*
who ate from the same bowl"
– Solzhenitsyn

We were poor, enjoyed no social status,
and Mother, motivated by what passes
as enlightenment, never failed to teach us
scorn for the barefoot, uneducated masses.
There was a category of the population,
they, she claimed to know: *they* were slackers,
trying always to rise above their station;
on ganja, dangerous machete attackers.
A bank note proffered on a black man's palm
must be infected, surely stolen. Scurrying
to the kitchen tap, she sanitizes her alarm,
the modern prototype of money laundering.

But no beggar for a drink was turned away,
water offered by a maid in a special glass
reserved for black lips. Forbidden to play
with black neighbours I was constrained to pass
long hours curled up in my imagination
which blazed from black and white to technicolour,
lifting to a poem, descending to depression,
lust waffling between hubris and terror.

My mother ran a canvas awning shop,
Aston, her chief sewer, deaf and dumb
from birth. She hired him from pity and to stop
moonlighting which sabotaged the trade, their medium
of communication grunts and signs.
He sits at his Singer machine among the desks
that crowd the factory floor, sewing hem designs

curving from the shuttle in graceful arabesques.
Aston, the black savant, could and did
calculate an awning's hypotenuse
as accurately and with the same *panache* as Euclid.
Rushing to judgment, Mother thought to accuse
him once of a mistake and, when it transpired
he was right, I witnessed the confrontation
in the sweltering shop between the hired
man and his mistress. How judge the allocation
of blame, the loss of face? They slowly advance
toward each other, the silent machines
holding their breaths and me as well, a dance
in which her arms are raised and he leans
forward, head bent. Then they embrace,
his cheek nestled against her breast, her fingers
caressing his Brillo hair – a moment of grace
that flickered only for a minute but still lingers.
Why slow applause from me? Such special care
deserved a special poem but I lacked the art
to craft it then. I attempt it here.
Mother, on this white page I cleanse my heart.

Black school mates were not allowed inside
our house so Joe and I would rendezvous
behind the garage, smoke cigarettes, allied
in our love for literature and art. In lieu
of comics we devoured Joyce and Miller.
Joe crafted stories bubbling with wit and laughter,
my *forte* metaphor, a faint poetic glimmer.
He dragged his exile to London where, after
the usual struggle, his third novel won
the Booker. "Let not thy soul be vexed,"
he wrote, "In life until you reach the colophon
there's hope. Your turn may yet be next."

Black schoolmates unwelcomed, but when Mother's
black doctor was summoned for an urgent visit,
a toilet usually acceptable for others
was attacked with scrub brush and Lysol, made fit
for the great man's ass. He enters like an African prince
come to bless a country cousin. She bares
her breasts for the kisses of the stethoscope, a wince
when his fingers massage her spine, hears
his consoling voice as he prepares the morphine
shot. When the heaving stops he stands
aside, slowly turns towards the pristine
bathroom to wipe her whiteness from his hands.
O brave, misguided one, necessity
is the mother of your contrition. Better
late than never! God will grab you willy-nilly,
leaving me behind, your rueful debtor.

Black skin! It enchants me every day,
warm to sight, a subtle colour to devote
a life of study. White skin seemed blah as if half way
through creation God forgot a second coat
of varnish to heighten tone. A Sunday painter, I broke
from landscapes to nudes, every jot and nipple
of the dermis under the microscope of brush.
I found a black model whose beauty stunned me.
When asked to pose nude she pursed her lush
lips, replied, "Only if you pay my fee."
It was outrageous but so was her body. "A mere tip,"
I bluffed. "My name is Hope and I despise white men.
Come the revolution be careful I don't slit
your slave-master throat. That said, when
do we start?" Hope was the epitome
of black beauty, warming my canvasses
with a glow that burned from memory
the cartel of whiteness; a glow that surpasses
in its subtlety the pale cheek

and bosom of the European nude
whose skin is white as goat's milk, weak
as the light empty bone china cups exude.
Ever eager to upstage me she warned one day
it was that time of month and I could see
the white string of her tampon on display
between her thighs. "I know," she volunteers,
"white men cannot bear very much reality.
If you are squeamish I will leave, but there's
still the little matter of my fee."

In an ex-colonial society servants
matter. Carmen entered our service fresh
from her village, a not-so-young applicant,
fearful of the city but, once in the mesh
of our love, catered to our domestic chores,
willing to cook, clean, wash, make
beds – on her knees to scrub the kitchen floor.
Her daily toil assuaged the ache
of our drudgery, made writing poems possible,
also dinner parties, playing chess.
Carmen's servanthood, more biblical
than secular, obliged me to assess
her status. As part of her apprenticeship
she mastered middle-class manners by example,
speech by imitation, her truth the deaconship
of our convictions, a chance for her to sample
our taste in art and music. In due course pregnant,
the father decamped for London and when her waters
broke it was my wife who led the chant
"Push, push" – me a reluctant *accoucheur*,
proud of the child Carmen christened Eunice.

The child, treated as one of our daughters, did
well enough at school. It was easy to dismiss
her sullenness as a teenage mask that hid

her inner turmoil. But at fifteen she confirmed
her pregnancy, father unknown. Carmen's heart
cracked with a remembered grief. I squirmed
in retrospect at my unsubtle part
in playing God, presumptuously uprooting
Eunice from her mother's nurturing soil, the ghetto
life she seemed to crave, her revolt the looting
of the treasury of good-will we had so
proudly gifted to her from the beginning.
Was it my misreading of the ethnic gene pool
that blighted the potential of the child's upbringing?
Eunice sleeps till noon refusing to return to school,
determined not to work, a troubled victim
of her blackness. We offer to relieve her pain
but stubbornly she sucks her teeth, that grim
island gesture of surrender and disdain.

I had married "Brown", one daughter "Black", so thought
that was that. *Quod erat demonstrandum!*
But the unhappy Carmen's case was fraught
with contradictions, my conscience numb.
We lodged her in our home with no regrets,
her uniforms hung in a bedroom next to ours,
on the bedside table a colour TV set
and bible; cut daily from the garden a vase of flowers.
Like marzipan scrolled on the cakes she baked,
her daily routine hardened into habit,
the tranquility of order. Time flaked
away her grief and I was able to acquit
myself of what remained of blame. But certain
bondages refuse to slacken, no
eating with us at table, her meals taken
in the kitchen, callalloo and sweet potato
dished from pot to mouth. Nor would she address us
by first name. I was "Da" for "Dad"
(invented by Eunice); my wife "Miss P" or "Missus";

yet she hugged us and for the children a chiliad
of kisses. After fifteen years Carmen accepts us
as mere mortals, part of a vaster
congregation of eccentrics. We had ordained
her to the rank of sisterhood, encouraged
to tweak the humdrum. At meals no one abstained
from comment, the dialectic space enlarged
with the "F" word and other such that cracked
across the silver like St. Elmo's fire.
Carmen, abashed at first, learned the knack
of feigned deafness, ignoring our vulgar choir.

A fart – that fast but simple leveller
of social *hubris* – with one high note
can interrupt a pompous speech, declare
finis to a formal dinner, an anecdote
that drags on too long. The accumulation
of gases in a gut is no respecter of class
or creed, subject only to the formulations
of Mr. Boyle and a hearty meal, alas!
Gathered in the kitchen we see Carmen bend
low to the gas stove, a dangerous position
for control of stomach acids. We offend
her by laughing, but before any inquisition
starts she stands and launches her defence.
After so many years in service she knows
the joke, blames any hint of flatulence
on the "dog", ending the imbroglio.
Thus, by a fart was sealed a vow to extol
our peccadilloes and our virtues, of sharing
secrets unique to us, a protocol
to banish embarrassment and blushes, swearing
to be human. On one occasion, Carmen's TV blaring
and her fast asleep for it was late,
I slipped quietly inside her room hearing
her steady breathing. From the TV screen delicate

pixel colours washed across her face:
pinks, lavenders, and blues, a fluid blending
that stippled her black skin. The urge to place
a kiss upon her forehead was overwhelming.

That night my room is redolent with the scent
of jasmine mated with mint. Rising from her couch
my muse, neither black nor white, a portent
of things to come, willing on oath to vouch
for my devotion to the craft, agrees
to sing again with me: harmonies
out of time but in the proper key.
A searching troop of tropes ensnares me;
poems, under the moving shadow of my pen,
compose themselves, claiming their pedigree
in foreign journals. But what I mostly crave
is the accord of my peers, black or white.
True poets abide their hearts and dispense
with ideology and cant. So when I had the sense
to ring the door bell, with seigniorial
grace they waved me in, welcoming me
into the holy circle of their communal
love, their respect affirmed and envy free –
Figs, Derek, Eddie, Mervyn, Wayne,
Louis, Ian, Earl, Gwyneth, Delores,
some bequeathing to the rest of us the pain
of their departures, the capriciousness
of death plucking now at my octogenarian
beard. These were happy halcyon days
earnest with art and the poetic struggle.
Guilt that gallops with whip and sharp spurs
has lost the race. I now dismount, able
at last to hang my hang-ups in the stable.

POEMS PREVIOUSLY PUBLISHED

From VIEW FROM MOUNT DIABLO (2003)

PROLOGUE

The light that I have so long loved turns
its gaze grudgingly from the old, romantic view
of islands, from the stubbled silver sheen of mountains
guarding valleys waking from their sleep, dew

overflowing the green uplifted chalice of a leaf,
dangling at each new morning's edge, testing
the gravity of calyx, bud and beaded stem;
turns from pious villages at night cupping

their candles in steep procession down a mountain path,
a girl's giggle muffled in the forest's throat;
turns, confused, from the embracing absolution of a
forgiving ocean washing away colonial guilt

like seaweed from a moon-glazed beach. Now the dream
is draining from the valley shadows, edges hardening
as the light changes to a harsh, uncompromising glare.
This day's sun is turning cynical, taking

its early morning tally in the tarnished air, a complacent
prison warder twisting a thumbprint into Kingston's face –
at high noon a hawk circles a laden
feeding tree, pure scrutiny without a trace

of insight, glint of a grin from the muzzle of a gun
as a black Clint Eastwood mocks the killing field
and runs that macho fable through another version.
This light scars the earth, a gaze held

unblinking to wither myth and drain the sap
from trees. Wordsworth could not survive a squint
at it. Pan the goat god has sworn allegiance
to the devil's party, swapped his simple flute

for an amplifier blasting fifteen hundred watts
but after all the raucous questions, a rumour
lingers, haunting the land, circulating a hiss
of whispers. In the city's bursting funeral parlours

the corpses glow at night, a nimbus of blue
acetylene burning the darkness under the roof,
lighting up the windows – crunch of bone and sinew
as a foot curls slowly into a cloven hoof.

To keep the awful secret, they are buried in their boots
but under the leather the light still glows, even
as coarse, animal hair begins to bristle
around the ankles, to sprout along the shins.

JAMAICA GOTHIC

Bevin, the butler, feared the sea, could not swim
but even after Independence he was proud to wear
the Spencer livery – white shirt, black tie, black shoes,
shiny black pants and, for proper atmosphere,

white gloves at meals. At the estate Great House
during his apprenticeship, he was an eager polisher
of family plate and silver shipped to the island
two hundred years ago, all trace of smear

shined off with chamois dipped in Goddard cleaner.
On Sundays he would stroll among the parked tractors
that hauled the cane carts, awesome even at rest –
his earnest dream, promotion to the pool of drivers.

On this Sunday, Spencer, his wife and guests
hunkered in the tepid water at the lawn's edge,
Bevin with a tray of gin and tonics pacing
the beach, mine host cajoling, "You need a nudge?

Can't you see we thirsty, boy?" Bevin prayed
for a brave heart but God was hard of hearing.
Slowly the water seeped into his shoes, damp
circles clamping his ankles, trousers sticking

to his shins. They lured him deeper in, laughter
gushing at his knees, the sea chucking his chin.
Then Spencer relented, grabbed the tray and spun him
spluttering back to land, back to a dry skin.

"Sorry you watch spoil, boy," Spencer slurred
at dinner, throwing a wad of dollars at his feet.
A gloved hand cupped the reward as Bevin
bowed, long practiced in the liturgy of retreat.

The next afternoon, Spencer's wife, bare breasted,
scampering from the sun deck to her room, bucked him up,
paused to flutter white fingers down his arm.
"We were drunk. A joke. No harm intended", the nap

of her contrition unruffled, her smile seductive.
She sauntered off into the setting sun,
the sea's silver slowly tarnishing to red.
The taut, unbroken line of the horizon

was thin as the lip of his machete that trimmed
the hedge outside her window, now the burning
bush that had singed the arm she touched. Time
longer than rope, he thought, the tide turning.

From MOVING ON (1998)

MISTER SON

Life funny fe true!
She call him "son", her only child,
And we servants add the "mister"
Not because him head is gold –
Look how it shine – but
Out of respeck and consolation
Fe what did happen.

After all, she come
From a good family
Dat did used to live at Cavaliers
Great House. But de fadder,
So anxious to keep de blood-stream pure,
So 'fraid a black man might catch her fancy,
Him send de gal a foreign fe study
Whiteness. And is a white man
Bruck down her door, yes.

But nobody 'round here talk
'Bout him after de marriage
Mash up and she come home wid de boy.
We get to understand
Him was a railway conductor,
One a de man dem who ride train,
Like from Kingston to Montego Bay
Dress in uniform collecting tickets.

She never marry again
And asthma rack she ches'
Like something block up her windpipe
And her heart. Is sick she sick fe true.

EARLY ENCOUNTER WITH THE BRITISH RAJ

A boy of ten, I knew them all,
all the Cockney NCOs
who wore short pants like me.
I was the regimental mascot.

The annual March Past
was the society function of the year,
tickets issued to the favoured few –
mostly white, a seasoning of browns.

A corporal was on duty when black Mr. Byrd,
pre-independence social provocateur,
bluffing for the cause in style,
drew up in a new 1937 Ford coupe
and tried to breach the gate.
"Do you know who I am?" he demanded.
"I am Byrd. Byrd, do you hear!"
The corporal whispered in reply,
"You could be a fucking 'awk, no one
gets in wifout a bleeding ticket."

Riding my donkey,
I violated military security at will.
I watched the troops assemble,
boots and rifle butts
slapping the asphalt, orders barked
in a hoarse scream as ranks were dressed.
In front a gaunt drum major
flung his silver baton in the air,
catching it behind his back.
Then the side drums and the bugles.
In the rear draped in a tiger skin,
a sergeant beat the great bass drum.

On the platform
guests shielded their eyes from the setting sun,
the Governor in a cockaded hat,
his aide-de-camp jingling with medals.

As the troops came into sight,
I slipped from ambush into the lead,
the donkey trotting briskly,
three mincing steps to each crash of the drum,
me riding bareback, feet dangling down,
behind me the voice of empire,
"Get out of it. Get out of it."
But I rode on, the battalion stretched behind.
"You little shit!" the drum major hissed,
missing a beat. And then
I heard what I have always craved,
O sweet colonial revenge,
laughter and the thunder of applause
as the Governor flashed me his salute,
the guests rising to their feet as one.

From GOOD-BYE ARISTOTLE, SO LONG AMERICA
(*Section VIII*)

On the head of a pin
thin Aristotle, fat Aquinas,
dancing, singing *find us, find us*,
the Scholastics all remind us
matter moves from potency to act
and thence, displaying modesty and tact,
by unaided human reason
we argue to the Beatific Vision.
After each syllogistic spree
we celebrate with Q.E.D.,
the logicians' victory shout
that leaves the grace, the mystery out.
If you want the end
then take the means – a simple rule
that separates the learned from the fool.
A tendency added to nature
is a habit, which ensures
that freedom of the will
remains unchallenged still.
Beauty is an entitative habit –
how wonderful in all the static
to encounter thought so arithmetic,
masturbation and a splendid bosom,
two petals of the habit blossom.

OUTSIDE THE ARTIST'S STUDIO

All during the crisis
the cat sat calmly
on the sofa inspecting
the medics and police,
a black spike splitting
the yellow O
of each eye floating in oil.

When the flash of a camera
flared, the gaze narrowed –
too slow to be a blink.
more a meditation –
like Vincent resting his eyes
before lifting the razor.

VIGIL

At the end of a hard day
dusk lurks in shadows
on a verandah overlooking Kingston,
an awning pulled up like the lid
of an eye afraid to blink.

The lights below flicker
like torches held by warriors
waiting to reclaim lost territory,
ready to creep forward
if the eyelid lowers.

Everything in front is flat, silent,
the lip of the sea and the lip of the sky
zip-locked at the horizon,
the empty wharves
sticking out their tongues.

At your back is a vast mountain,
hunched like a vulture over the house,
waiting for what will happen –
a prayer half uttered
sliced in two by an avenging knife,
what could be affirmed
choked off at the very thought of it.

THE GARDEN

Welcome! You think the bamboo stand
more lush this year? You have an eye.
The people perish daily yet the island
blooms. The blood of those who die

seems to enrich the soil and roses darken
to a warmer red, crotons
to a deeper gold. How else explain the garden's
new exuberance? Tonight the guns

will fertilize a lovelier tomorrow
while I stroll in splendid isolation
under the protection and shadow
of this wall, finding consolation

in music, poetry and art. After all,
I do not pull the trigger, harbour no hate.
How fey of you, my dear, to smuggle this apple
past the customs. May I take a bite?

A DEATH IN THE FAMILY

On her last birthday she blew out
thirty candles and her brother,
despite his stammer, raised a toast,
confessing she was a stronger swimmer,
ran a faster mile. "But in the b-bush
I was the b-better shot. You closed both eyes."

Now, gnawed thin by cancer
the doctors wash their hands
and send her home to plan the details of her dying.
For her ashes, a disk of gold –
yellow interspersed with cobalt splashes.
The custom casket, round as the sun,
is fired for her at the school of art
and like a resplendent vase
flowers from her bedside table, admired
by all who come to visit and to praise
her fortitude. "Scatter me from a hill,"
she commands and writes her will.

But on the day the breeze is gusting
and the ashes, shaken from the urn, behave
the way that ashes will in a wind,
bits of the deceased flying
in the mourner's faces, blotching
their lapels and blouses. Her brother
grabs the disk and leads them
to an abandoned garden
where a skeet machine crouches
like a praying mantis on the mountain's back.

He cocks the iron arm, the spring compressing,
fits the clay container in the rusting track
and pulls the lever. With a great hissing

the disk whirls up, spinning over the valley.
“F-fly, f-fly!” her brother cries, aligning
thumb and finger like a gun. At its apogee
the vase explodes and out of the fragments
of her last command the ashes drift slowly down.
The procession turns and stammers back
to the cold cars and the broil of town.

THIRD WORLD

High rise hotels, concrete shoulders thrown back,
stand like soldiers self-consciously at attention
while round their boots this third world city sprawls.

How reconcile such rectangularity
with the random chance from which it springs,
such stoic silence with the rhetoric of politicians

and bougainvilleas practising their purple patches?
Minibuses, alias "Cisco Kid" and "Black Ben Hur"
bully their rights of passage

through barefoot handcart boys burning calluses for brakes.
Drooping high tension lines, drunk with power,
play "cat in the cradle" with their cables.

Fences out of plumb lurch like drunker sailors to the sea.
Even the horizon bent.
No wonder our foreign policy is nonaligned

MOUNTAIN TIME

This mountain dips down
like the graph of my desire
into the hot harbour.
An old voyeur
I sit sweating under the shingled armpit
of a fake Mansard roof
remembering Cezanne's brush with Sainte Victoire
which lasted fifteen years.
Was he intemperate?

Stubbled with trees, my mountain
shines like serge in silver light,
the mid-morning sun burning
as once I burned.
An imperial palm, surrendering,
folds down its umbrella.
The mountain yawns and stretches,
tired of posing, shameless as earth.
All other lusts but looking have leached away.

Like Cezanne behind his easel,
one arm extended in the classic painter's stance,
plumbing the horizon with the handle of the brush,
scaling distance with a thumb,
I have learned to measure grandeur with a squint,
moiety of all those mountains
even faith can't move.

A LONG PRODUCTIVE LIFE

"Come, O you black daughters of Jerusalem!"
A groan.
"Thy breasts are clusters of grapes."
Another groan.
"Thy hair is a flock of goats."
"Is she-goat you take me for?" she railed,
flouncing from the bed.

He was a black country parson
with a self-conferred Doctor of Divinity degree –
despoiling virgins a perk of the profession.
The psalms seduced him,
those smouldering simple words
he could not fathom.

To avoid exposure as a charlatan
demanded bible study of an earnest sort
and once committed to the fraud
he kept up with the learning.

"Thy two breasts are like two young roes –
What is a roe? A hind?
A milk white hind..."
By Christmas he had finished Dryden
and the mainstream church;
five more years for Paul,
the paranoia and the passion of the man;
three years for the book of Job,
that eternal brawl without a winner;
another decade to master Greek and Hebrew
before tackling Revelations and the Apocalypse.

The government of Israel,
recognising third world talent
tendered two first-class tickets to Tel-Aviv.
He cashed in one,
pocketing the proceeds, and on arrival
struck up a friendship with a Sabra.
"Thy hair is like a flock of goats,"
he quoted. "Don't be ridiculous,"
she laughed, grabbed her Uzi and departed.

He outlived his enemies
and died at ninety-five.
The nurse, her hair in cane rows,
leaned to the rattle in his chest,
her braids brushing his face.
"Thy hair is like a flock of goats,"
he croaked, lifting his head.
"What a lovely sentiment," she agreed
and watched him die content.

CAPRICORN

First a frog pinned on its back
in a dissecting tray, split
down the belly, heart still pulsing,
the biology master explaining
what makes it tick;
then a bleating kid with sad
Byzantine eyes resisting slaughter
and I'm on my feet protesting
through tears, Tarpey and Granger
sniggering in the back row,
but I'm beyond their Third Form scorn
sobbing in full flood.
"Science – not murder," the priest insists
but to calm the crisis suggests
I take it home. I name him Giles –
my waif, my ward who shares
survival with me, real or sham,
frolicking through the house
on delicate hoofs, skidding on the tiles.
He sleeps beside my bed, head
twisted back flat on his shoulder
pretending to be a sacrificial lamb.

But Giles outgrows me to full ramhood.
While I inspect my sparse pubic hair,
he has sprouted horns and beard,
a lean pink penis and enormous oblong balls.
Tethered now, I squat
to pet him and he attacks
my knee, humping it, the air
heavy with the semen salt of goat.
I turn my back on him
and when they pick me up

a butt bruise stains my thigh,
Giles head high snorting with lewd
panache. So much for gratitude!
I limp out of the lesson
of his gaze to a closet where
a rusty dissecting tray resides.

GOOD FRIDAY IN A TOURIST TOWN

On this nude beach no drops of blood soil
the whiteness of the sand, no sombre shadows cross
the naked bodies of tourists sprawled on towels,
still as statues, pretending death. In honour
of the day a local radio station plays
Handel's "Messiah", the London Philharmonic
drowned by a chorus of dissenting waves,
a fringe of palm trees swaying their heads in protest,
"No, no", until the tape is changed.
Then the wail of Marley's "No Woman, No Cry"
and suddenly even here it is Good Friday.

HIC EST

The first assault stains
the beach with blood,
the priest's mixed
with the dead and dying troops.
An antiseptic moon cools the bodies
he is too weak now to bless.
His right hand twitches
and a sniper fires, another
bullet boring the upturned
palm, more blood
from this stigmata
oozing into sand.

At first light another
wave of troops looms
out of the mist, tanks
rampaging through the bodies,
his other hand caught in a coiling tread.
A week later on the hospital ship,
in a daze of anaesthetic,
a surgeon explains why
the amputations saved
his life, the left arm
below the shoulder, the right
midway between wrist and elbow.

Hope rebuilds itself
like the muscles in his upper arms
and back, trained for two years
at his will to twitch, stretch,
roll, pull, bulge, contract.
Prosthesis strapped to stumps
under the alb, he bends over

the paten, sucks in
a deep breath, hears
the servo motors humming
in the artificial joints,
sensors sensing,
hydraulic fluids flushing
as he slightly shrugs

a message to the muscles.
The silver arm edges
forward, the tapered
titanium tips a fraction open.
The lips of the claw nudge
the Host, closing on it
like a kiss, lifting it
as the bell tinkles. He smiles,
mumbles in Latin *Deus ex machina,*
his private joke.

HISTORY ANYONE?

Here they come –
generals blowing their own trumpets,
lawyers clad in their briefs,
politicians
bloated with promises,
priests
bent under their crosses,
businessmen holding ledgers
high over their heads
like trophies,
poets
dipping quills
in wine-dark swirls.

They swarm Mecca and Jerusalem
and the ayatollahs and the rabbis
each grabs an edge of history
until it rips in half;
in Hyderabad
they shake all the hands
of Buddha and history, like smoke,
drifts from the funeral pyres;
they track through Africa
trampling the Serengeti and savannahs
and an elephant remembers,
"This is our history";
they send slaves to the Caribbean
and a black scholar stooped with tenure, sighs,
"We have no history";
they drive the feathered warriors
before them down the trail of tears
and Chief "He who Weeps"
bellows at bingo on the reservation,
"Eleven – Betty Grable's legs.
This is our history."

STEPHANIE

Stephanie, on the run,
gives no quarter, asks for none,
insists, “Don’t make a fuss,
a quiet dinner, just the boys and us.
With inflation, a big expense
cannot be justified, does not make sense.”

My child, what has sense to do with it?

We who write poems know
how grudgingly our true emotions flow,
insisting that the stress of line and living
leaves little time for ritual thanksgiving.

I know a modern girl like you would not be happy
with something sentimental, soppy.
But underneath, it well could be
you cherish celebration as much as we.

So having cracked the prudence barrier,
enjoy your birthday, make it happier
with excess. After four decades
push now comes to shove:
a father’s fond advice –
discount the cents and bank the love.

From THE DENTING OF A WAVE (1992)

CARPENTERS

Years ago when I had nothing else to do
except to ogle back at tree ghosts in a forest
about a mile along the road from Hardwar Gap,
my friend, Malcolm, who had long inhabited
a shack that rotted in the ferns and bracken bush
undertook to build a one-room timber house
and to this end employed the services and skills
of Mr. Coombs, a carpenter from Silverhill.

I was ten, Malcolm incalculably old
and purple black. I was nearly white
but now I know we shared a rare astonishment –
he at the prospect of a house respectable
enough in which to die and me at Mr. Coombs
pegging out a new domain with such casual
grace and squint-eyed wisdom as Penn & Venables
would have envied, albeit this forest colony
was twelve by sixteen feet of mildewed mulch.

Pencil tucked behind his ear, Mr. Coombs
bends over a beam bridging two inverted
forty-gallon drums – its yellow fur erect, ready
for the razor tongue of plane to shave its splinters,
to peel its skin down to the smell of pine and pitch
while Mr. Coombs up to his unlaced boots in clay
whistles through gold-capped teeth, blessing with
flicks of sweat the curtilage of Malcolm's plot.

Then, hand over hand, columns are raised and braced.
Hammer strokes explode the silver heads of nails
and every time the carpenter's right arm shoots up
I blink, never knowing if the sparks I see –
red and blue – are real or only in my head.

Mr. Coombs plucks a chalked cord like a taut
harp string, aligning horizontals on the soil's
black skin. Swinging a piece of twine tied to a rock
he sights for honest perpendiculars.

While Mr. Coombs lays down the floor and Malcolm
cuts rubber strips from an abandoned tyre to hinge
the door (rubber like silence does not rust in woods)
I am allowed the apprenticeship of scraps.
With two lengths of surplus laths and rusty nails
I make the primal shape, only slightly
out of true but right enough for showing off.

In eight weeks Malcolm takes possession of his
home, celebrating title and completion
with Mr. Coombs and a bottle of white rum.
I am invited in, noticing the warmth
of timbered in-ness. Hardly listening to the drift
of their postmortem, I choose the toolbox as my stool
pondering the career of carpenters.

ABLUTIONS

A pipe jutted like a gibbet
from the outside kitchen wall above a shallow
cistern and when in the cool of early schoolboy
mornings its silver rope of water whipped
its chill around my throat, choking off
the involuntary scream, I wondered
why poverty ordained such ritual
ablutions and, anointing crotch with red
carbolic soap, cherished a hope the girl
next door would peek around the corner
pretending indignation.

I claimed this time and place by right of water
and since the world still slept I willed that she
should float naked across the fence and lift a foot
into the cistern. I watched the water runnel
from her breasts, flowing into a new
and nervous valley, beading the pubic hair
with pearls. Then she was gone
and I, mouth salivaless and dry,
walked on heels across the dusty yard
back into the snoring house.

It seems so long ago, those days of cold ablutions,
their rapture stamped upon my memory
like the pattern of a fern on skin –
pain and pleasure wired in a silver circuit
of fusion and confusion,
passion and compassion and the rueful knowledge
that since my sudsing took a richer
turn I have scrubbed away the coin of her face.

Could what they say about
cold showers still be true
if this poem only tingles into life
at the remembered shock of early morning water?

HARBOUR VIEW

Beyond the edge of my window
overlooking the harbour
the prow of a red cargo boat
floats without motion
on the blue water.

The steel hull is smooth
and looms immovable above
the agitated
surface of the sea surrounding it.

No one part, neither the longitude of the boat,
the nervous petulance of the water
nor the colour of each
is strong enough to break the tension
of the picture's composition
locked into the frame of the window.

But it will not last.
Either the ship,
eaten up with demurrage,
will sink or sail
or the sea,
in conspiracy with the wind,
will push the red prow back
and thus prevail,
or I, unable to be a witness to defeat
will close the curtain.

JAMAICA FAREWELL

What I remember
is the sun-crazed summer
that you said good-bye,
light filed to the fine
fury of a machete
slicing open the eye
of the sea, slashing at our faces
as we drove across the city
to the airport.

"Why am I going,
genes or geography?"
you asked, tracing an alien
map with your fingers
on my cheek. Even without tears
its borders blurred and disappeared.

An indifferent Kingston
flushed itself into the harbour
silting up the ocean
with departures. The road
curled to the airport
like a question mark,
its meagre wrist of land
as fragile as your embracing hands.

WAITING

(For Doreen)

The bedside lamp splashes
your side of the room with light,
tracing the mould of your body
in the vacant bed,
filling the pillow's depression
and the pores of the chenille spread
with the scent of your elbows.

Your glasses, slightly out of shape,
pretend to read the open book
on which they rest,
making an empty spectacle of themselves
in the absence of your eyes.

On the bedside table
the telephone, silent and tense,
holds a hand over its mouth.

Goodnight when you come home!

I have missed you
as if you were away
for a long time
during which I grew interminably old
waiting for your return –
afraid to shut off the light.

TIME AND TIDE

Between the V of the hull
and the XXXs of the verandahed villas
lies the blue sea talking to itself
in ultramarine tautologies,
each syllable a wave
foaming into gibberish upon the reef.

To port is Cuba
and the terror of a navigational error,
to starboard
the headlands of Port Antonio
like a beached whale
wallowing in shallow water.

Crossing the reef we run aground,
knocking the engine out.
In that instant of stunned silence
the coral claims its right of encrustation,
secreting new monuments for another generation –
the jeweled oval of my wife's astonished
mouth, my son's bronzed back
bent over the dead wheel,
my daughter's arms, ripening to jade
locked around her sons,
my right hand, wrist manacled in sand,
groping for the log book and a pen.

HE KNOWS WHAT HEIGHT IS

He knows what height is, this hillside dweller
who squints occasionally at the waving sea
below, the lustre of its greener
eye engulfing the valley to return his gaze.
One day hacking at high vines
he saw a shape like his cutlass hanging in the sky,
motionless, an off-course Air Jamaica
plane aimed at the airport. He has never
flown, assumes that those who do by looking down
can bless or cast a spell upon the ground.

High is the axed pine that pitches forward
shivering like a compass needle in the circle
of the clearing, pulled true north to where the bird,
a solitaire – like him a mountain exile,
flutes its two-note elegy, centre
of lamentation in which his hut is huddled.
At dusk he slides down the slope from field
to shack, leaning back against the incline,
heels hugging dirt, a trickle of stones
rolling before him into the ravine.

He sits alone at sunset, the hills hunched
around him leaking purple, the black crack
of the gorge narrowing to a scar stitched
into the mountain's back. Clinging to the brink
of the precipice his hut is a wattled
blink of lantern light behind
the streaming banners of the evening mist.

At another time, another edge, he watched
his mother climb a guinep tree, skirt
billowing in the breeze and from a limb

lower a swing for him, sisal knotted
under a wooden slat. Higher and higher
she pushed him into terrifying air.
A bird floated down the mountain, riding
high currents over the ridges.

He felt it swinging
him between the peaks, feet dangling
above the abyss filling up with shadows,
elbows screaming at his sides,
fingers frozen on the fog frayed vines.
As it was in the beginning so, after all
these years, the sign and wonder – between his legs
the anus closing, the shrinking of the balls.

DEATH OF A HONDA RIDER

From a pothole's asphalt vase
a sprig of red hibiscus waves
the traffic off. A Honda rider,
knees splayed, grinning his route
through black self-generated air
floats his teeth across the windscreen
of our car in hot pursuit
of someone he desires or despises
more than us, the butt
of a revolver tucked into his belt
under the billowing shirt.

How soon before they stumble on his body
in a gully, the front wheel
of the Honda spinning slowly,
the engine ticking as it cools?

Air palpable as oil
from the crank case lubricates
the black descending of the crows.
Whatever dreams he dreams lying on his back
still exact the rictus smile
that lashed the corners of his mouth
to the centre of his skull
where, under Rasta locks, his truth
is hidden and a million
revelations, spliff certified,
flares to a faith you could not face
Unless you dared to ride the pillion.

SILENCE

When the accustomed hum which I
have long accepted as the absence
of sound suddenly ceases, the
ensuing silence pours into
my ears like syrup and I become
profoundly deaf.

I have not heard,
oh Lord, the lamentation of
the poor, nor the laughter of
the rich. Nor in my sojourn
in foreign lands has the echo
of the bud unfolding to a rose
disturbed my sleep.

The summer season
washes across my history
like a sable brush loaded
with water blurring the boundaries
of exact events. I do not hear their consequences
being watered down.

By December
the sky cracks and out of its fissures
a cold wind swirls, stripping
the leaves from their branches. They drop
like black tears into the gutters
of cities but I am not awakened
by the splash of their weeping.

Age spots
map their dominion on the back of my hands
and a voice whispers through the syrup

"When you are old and your soul is shivering,
the last stitch of its dream unravelling,
pull this poem like a shawl
around your nakedness. Only
the rags of words are left to warm
the marrow, once more the word made flesh.

From MR. GOODMAN'S LAST VISIT ABROAD

He found her dead
stretched upon the Persian carpet
in the apartment,
the red skirt,
an outflung hand,
the shattered heart
now part of a new design –
from heaven's height
a small carpet stain.
Her eyes and mouth
were open, her lips
quite blue as were her fingertips,
cold to the touch.

He shut her eyes
pressing on the lids
but the mouth refused to close,
cheek muscles slack.
If there was thread
he would have stitched
the lips into a smile.
He rummaged through a drawer –
threadbare – only a dictionary,
Webster's unabridged,
which he reposed upon her breast,
words enough to wish her rest
and to prop the jaw.

FLORIDA

I am walking in a subdivision
dubbed “The Elms” in which there are no
trees and the houses line the street in

fenceless duplication, so anxious to avoid
the sweat of living, all their dust and draft
are packed in garbage pans equipped with

wheels. Outside the kitchen walls, air-conditioners
crouch like frogs on concrete pads
croaking in the morning heat. At one

corner a red-bowlered fire hydrant
impersonates Toulouse-Lautrec guarding a
newspaper wrapped in a condom

of cellophane. At another corner, a flaccid
American flag, *pro bono publico*,
is shafted by a thin aluminum pole.

The doors of the garages lift open
on command, saying “Aah” for the inspection
of tools aligned like teeth along the walls.

Yesterday the kids were playing hopscotch
on the sidewalk and in one square
a red tricycle gleams

like a triumphant taw.
It could have been a red wheel barrow
but this is not the

Patterson geography.
Only the black barrels
engorged with garbage roll.

THE VIRGIN MARY AT WELLESLEY COLLEGE

(for Elizabeth)

Our daughter back home after a year
in Paris where we had visited with her
to celebrate her twenty-first,
had met her beau,
all four holding hands and dancing
down the hill from *Sacre Coeur*,
reminds us now in a quiet interlude
after coffee and cognac,
her laugh like a demure arpeggio,
of the time when she was eight years old
and the Virgin Mary appeared to her
sitting on the Formica top
of the built-in dressing table –
not your classic face but a sweet smile,
tres triste, and the hushed imperative
about the curve her destiny might take.

Then that laugh again sliding up the scale
and the confession that in her freshman year
at Wellesley, suddenly stricken
with pneumonia, alone in the infirmary
fighting not to drown in her own lungs,
she prayed to Mary
and when she woke up in the morning
the odour of disinfectants
had evaporated and the perfume of roses
blossomed in the ward
filling it with new sweet air
which she was able to inhale
but which the nurse,
because her sinuses were blocked,
could not detect.

There was this long, half awkward silence
as under the magnification of beginning tears
her hazel eyes grew larger;
then the laugh again
and I thought that she –
undeniably touched –
should be writing this poem

SUFFICIENCIES

I think only as deep as puzzlement,
I feel but only to the edge of pain.

My fear extends
no further than the shadow
that bends a corner.

My tears are equal to my grief,
my ears no sharper than a sound.

My legs are long enough, but only just,
to touch the ground.

MY GOD

The divine mind
Contemplates the infinite will,
Defines it in finite form
And time and space
Become caesuras in the long line that poems forth,
The nib of the poised pen
Still wet with words. Time
Is space unravelling and space
Is the time it takes to trace the limits
Which the pen has shaped.

To be infinite is to contain
All contradiction –
Love and indignation,
Power and submission.
Life and death.
But not repose.
God at the switch!
If he should doze
The energy of containment would explode,
Blow up creation,
Time and space echoing back to silence.
Homer nods
But not my God scripting his metaphors,
The poised pen descending.

CAVAFY AT TERRA NOVA

Cavafy sat in his spats at Terra Nova
his white suit tailored
from a large table cloth
peeled of the pearl of its damask,
watching a tight-bottomed busboy
serving a couple of tourists.

Everyone else had abandoned their stations.
The Captain who for years
buried his tips in a tin can
to avoid paying taxes
was digging furiously in the garden
to recapture his cache.

Cooks postponed soaking plum puddings
and although not a war cry was throated
farmers prepared for the scorching of crops
crouching like relay runners
waiting for rumours and matches.

Businessmen cremated their minute books
anxious to face new eras
with clean hands and ledgers.
A number of sage civil servants
blew out their brains with unsuspected flair
while priests high and low
consumed their wafers in fear
of the advancing host.

When the tight-assed busboy,
serving soup with trembling hands,
asked Cavafy what was wrong,
were the barbarians coming after all,

Cavafy dabbed his lips and sighed,
recalling that some time ago
he had composed a small piece
which might be apropos.

He had a copy in his valise
which, after dinner, if the boy
was really interested
he would be happy to explain.

Cavafy sat in his spats in a corner,
the busboy beside him like a question mark,
the room's remainder
a still life of tables
without spoons or plates
reserved for the late arrival of barbarians.

LEDA

Why are we,
black daughters of Jamaica,
so afraid of lizards?
Confronted by such a wall
of prejudice I think
that they, the bloodless ones,
have climbed it with aplomb.

I have seen
some fall, of course, but only
rarely and even then
they rise with grace to the occasion,
sticking out their tongues
in half-amused contempt.

The angled head,
the hooded ackee eyes,
ancestral lineaments
inherited from one
who scaled a garden wall
and gazing at a naked lady
felt the world's first blush
blistering his skin.

White girls deserve
unruffled long-necked swans.
Under a poinciana tree
I keep a crimson assignation.
With a parting of the leaves he comes
and in the red shade,
this other Eve, breasts tightening,
is only half afraid.

ABOUT THE AUTHOR

Ralph Thompson has published three previous collections of poetry: *The Denting of a Wave* (1992), *Moving On* (1998) and *View from Mount Diablo* (2003), and an annotated edition in 2009. This verse novel won the 2001 Jamaica National Literary competition and has been taught at the University of the West Indies.

The son of a Jamaican mother and an American father, Ralph Thompson was educated in Jamaica at St George's College and in America at Fordham University and at the Fordham School of Law where he earned a *Doctor Juris* degree. He is a former member of the New York Bar and served as a JAG officer in the US Air Force stationed in Japan for two years during the Korean conflict.

On his return to Jamaica in 1954 he started a career as a businessman, painter and poet. He has served as the managing director of two major companies quoted on the Jamaican stock exchange. In 1976 an exhibition of his paintings was favourably reviewed and more recently his work has been featured in Jacqueline Bishop's *Writers Who Paint, Painters Who Write*. He has served on the Jamaican National Council on Education and the Early Childhood Commission, and was awarded the CD (Commander of Distinction) for public service in the Jamaican National Honours of 1988.

Married and with four children, Ralph Thompson lives with his wife in Kingston.

PROFESSOR EDWARD BAUGH

Edward Baugh is a distinguished Jamaican poet, orator, scholar and author of critical and biographical works on Derek Walcott and Frank Collymore. He is Professor Emeritus at the University of the West Indies.

ALSO BY RALPH THOMPSON

The Denting of a Wave
ISBN: 9780948833625; pp. 88; pub. 1993; price: £7.99

These poems are the fruits of a maturity which has learned to confront the facts of life and death with both exuberance and dread. Humane and finely crafted, his poems are firmly rooted in Caribbean particularity, but are universal in their concerns. He has the story-teller's gift which grips, then leaves the reader pondering on the subtleties beneath the surface.

Moving On
ISBN: 9781900715171; pp. 104; pub. 1998; price: £8.99

The poems in *Moving On* recreate moments of change, loss and epiphany. There are vivid glimpses of a prewar Jamaican childhood – of sexual discovery and of the rude ingratitude of a goat. The long sequence, "Goodbye Aristotle, So Long America", explores the years of study at a Jesuit university in America and the making both of a lifetime's values and of the sense of irony which has made it possible to live with them. Other poems reflect on the experience of ageing, of increasing vulnerability, but also of an increased appreciation for what sustains human relationships through time.

View from Mount Diablo, annotated edition
ISBN: 9781845231446; pp. 160; pub. 2009; price: £12.99

'*View from Mount Diablo* is a remarkable achievement. Its knowledge of the island, the entwining of private lives and politics, lifts Jamaican poetry to a level that has not been attempted before. The poetry is strong, imaginative, fascinating in detail. It describes terrible things with understatement, yet with compassion. I don't think anything could be more harrowing than the rape of Chantal, or the boy begging Alexander to spare his life... This is narrative poetry at its best. Not only Jamaicans, but I think readers in England and the USA, will appreciate this book. It is something new.' Louis Simpson

This fully annotated edition, edited by John Lennard, offers a full introduction situating Thompson's Jamaican National Literary Award-winning verse-novel in its formal, Caribbean, and global contexts, and provides detailed notes explicating background history, real events transposed into fiction, and the skilled foreshortening that maps an individual life onto a national calamity.